Contents

shaping
the new
NHS

CAN MARKET FORCES
BE USED FOR GOOD?

JENNIFER DIXON, JULIAN LE GRAND AND PETER SMITH

The King's Fund is an independent charitable foundation working for better health, especially in London. We carry out research, policy analysis and development activities, working on our own, in partnerships, and through grants. We are a major resource to people working in health, offering leadership and education courses; seminars and workshops; publications; information and library services; and conference and meeting facilities.

Published by
King's Fund
11–13 Cavendish Square
London W1G 0AN
www.kingsfund.org.uk

© King's Fund 2003

Charity registration number: 207401

First published 2003

ISBN 1 85717 477 1

Priced copies available from:

King's Fund Bookshop
11–13 Cavendish Square
London W1G 0AN
Tel: 020 7307 2591
Fax: 020 7307 2801
www.kingsfundbookshop.org.uk

Free download available from: www.kingsfund.org

Edited by Eleanor Stanley
Cover design by Minuche Mazumdar Farrar
Printed and bound in Great Britain

About the authors

Jennifer Dixon
Director of Health Policy at the King's Fund, with particular responsibility for analysis of NHS workforce issues and the future shape of the NHS

Jennifer's background is in clinical medicine and health services research. From 1998 to 2000, she was policy advisor to the Chief Executive of the National Health Service, Sir Alan Langlands. In 1990, she studied the US health care system at first hand as a Harkness Fellow. She has written widely on health care reform in the UK and abroad, and is currently working with colleagues at the King's Fund analysing the lessons that can be learned by the NHS from managed care organisations in the USA.

Julian Le Grand
Richard Titmuss Professor of Social Policy at the London School of Economics, and King's Fund Senior Associate

Julian is the author, co-author or editor of 12 books and over 90 articles and book chapters on public policy, including health policy. He has acted as an advisor and consultant on health policy, welfare policy and social exclusion to the World Bank, the European Commission, the World Health Organization, the Cabinet Office, HM Treasury, the UK Departments of Health and Social Security, and the National Audit Office. He was a member of the Fabian Commission on Taxation and Citizenship, and the Institute of Public Policy Research Commission on Public/Private Partnerships, and has acted as a non-executive director of a Family Health Service Authority and a Health Commission, and as the Vice-Chair of an NHS trust. He is currently a Commissioner on the Commission for Health Improvement. He appears frequently on radio and television, and writes regularly for the press.

Peter Smith

Professor of Economics at the Centre for Health Economics at the University of York

Peter's research interests include the financing, efficiency and performance management of public services, topics on which he has published widely. He has designed several major systems of formula funding currently in operation in the UK public sector, and has been a member of numerous government advisory committees, including the Department of Health's Advisory Committee on Resource Allocation and the Treasury's Performance Information Panel. He has also acted as a consultant to many other national and international agencies, including the Organisation for Economic Co-operation and Development, the World Health Organization and the World Bank, and currently holds a three-year fellowship from the Economic and Social Research Council.

Foreword

The NHS Plan (2001) set out the Government's ambitious ten-year reform programme for the health service – a vision it went on to back with unprecedented increases in funding. But as planning has given way to implementation, it has become clear how difficult it is to deliver tangible improvements on the ground, which raises wider questions about how effective organisational change in public services can be achieved.

How to improve the quality, efficiency and accessibility of health services remain central questions facing all governments in developed countries. In the UK, some policy initiatives – for example, waiting list targets or local authorities fines for 'bed-blocking' – imply improvements will spring from greater central control. Others – such as foundation trusts or the expansion of patient choice – seem to assume mechanisms such as local competition or consumer demand are the key to change.

So no single approach seems to be shaping the Government's health policies. If the Government's mantra is 'what counts is what works', will such pragmatism prove effective? Can a highly centralised approach on the one hand and a market-led appraoch on the other sit comfortably side by side?

Policy makers and professionals alike need an informed, transparent debate on the shape of the new NHS. What are the real trade-offs between, for example, equity of access and greater patient choice? Will market forces provide an effective response to the growing demands on health and social care services made by an ageing population? Is there a need for an 'arm's length' NHS agency that separates central policy and local planning?

At the same time, recent disputes about GPs' and consultants' contracts raise further important questions. What kinds of professional roles and skills are needed to underpin a modern health service? Are professional values – the cornerstone of the old NHS – taking a beating? Will they change or collapse?

Shaping the New NHS: Can market forces be used for good? draws on a recent King's Fund breakfast debate, which presented the views of three seasoned commentators (Jennifer Dixon, Julian Le Grand and Peter Smith) on the issue of competition and choice in the new NHS. It examines the case for and against internal markets in the health sector, and asks whether it is possible to combine the best of market disciplines with planned provision by differentiating between types of demand.

This discussion paper launches a wider King's Fund Shaping the New NHS programme of research, seminars, debates and publications, which will run throughout 2003. It builds on earlier work carried out in 2001, which brought together a group of professionals, commentators and academics from health care and beyond, chaired by Lord Haskins, broadly to consider key issues facing the NHS. They pinpointed three immediate and inter-related problems: over-politicisation; excessive centralisation; and lack of responsiveness to individuals and communities.

Their thoughts, published in January 2002 as *The Future of the NHS: A framework for debate*, attracted widespread interest and media coverage. I hope you will find this paper and its scrutiny of market forces helpful and illuminating in its look at one strand of the debate.

Julia Neuberger
Chief Executive, the King's Fund
May 2003

Summary

■ Despite a plethora of Government policy initiatives to effect
transformational change in the NHS – now backed by substantial
investment – there is a growing perception that improvements are
taking place too slowly. How can the Government accelerate change
and make services more responsive to patients in the way the public
increasingly expects?

■ Much of the debate has focused on whether, and how, sharper
market incentives might prompt better performance, and whether
we will witness a return to previous experiments with internal
markets. It remains difficult to discern a single, coherent approach
to Government health policy, suggesting a largely instrumental
view of the role of central control versus local market forces.

■ Any new use of market forces is likely to be markedly different from
previous experiments. On the policy front, it is clear that:
  - competition between providers will be based on quality,
    not price
  - there will be a standard set of national prices
  - patient choice of secondary care provider is being encouraged
  - money will flow around the NHS in ways that support and
    encourage competition
  - new providers will be able to enter the NHS market.
  The health care environment has also changed:
  - information systems and data are much improved
  - the system of regulation and standard setting is better.

■ Would a 'market', initially between NHS trusts, work any better
than when tried in 1991? Should it be tried again? This paper, which
includes contributions from two senior economists in health care,
and the director of health policy at the King's Fund, debates
these questions.

■ Julian Le Grand supports the introduction of stronger market incentives to prompt improved performance among secondary care providers. He:
  - notes the positive effect market incentives have had in primary schools
  - argues that new structures (such as new systems of regulation and performance measurement) will help minimise undesirable consequences
  - suggests that, in 1991, the NHS internal market did not work as intended because incentives were not strong enough, and objectives were not aligned between hospital consultants and managers
  - advocates the use of stronger financial incentives to remunerate hospital consultants – for example, payment on a fee-for-service basis to encourage greater productivity.

■ Peter Smith does not support even modest experimentation with stronger market incentives. He:
  - notes the adverse effects that market incentives can produce in health care
  - argues that, despite the new structures put in place since 1997, a key check on the adverse effects of stronger market incentives is the professional ethic
  - suggests that market disciplines could seriously undermine this ethic, resulting in poorer quality care and health outcomes for patients (particularly those with chronic medical problems, rather than those requiring straightforward non-emergency surgery)
  - believes that a more competitive market between secondary care providers risks focusing managers' attention on the acute sector (in particular, elective care) at the expense of the non-acute.

■ Jennifer Dixon asks whether it is possible to combine the best of market disciplines with planned provision by differentiating between types of demand. She:

- – agrees with Peter Smith that discussions about market forces in health care often focus on secondary care – in particular, elective care
- – argues that the most complex, challenging and costly conditions to treat are chronic medical conditions
- – believes that the structure, organisation and incentives appropriate for the optimal treatment of these conditions may be very different from those for elective care
- – suggests that a market split between secondary care providers and purchasers, with competition between providers, may not result in the best care for patients requiring complex and integrated care.

■ Perhaps a 'fork in the road' is now possible, with elective (surgical) care provided by competing hospitals, and other forms of care stimulated by more appropriate incentives. New conceptions of a 'market' in the NHS may emerge – allowing more vertical integration between primary and secondary care providers.

■ In the medium term, it is clear that:
- – the Government will encourage more providers and greater patient choice of provider within the NHS over the next few years
- – the health care environment will be dynamic and changeable, as new opportunities arise from the external environment and from new policies.

■ In the short term:
- – the pace and scope of change is likely to be dominated by the ability of the NHS to achieve the targets set out in the NHS Plan, and the next general election
- – If Labour is re-elected, and the NHS is not perceived to be changing fast enough, then pressure will grow to introduce stronger market incentives on the provider side and, ultimately, on the demand side.

Framing the debate

Slow progress on modernisation

The Government faces a difficult problem. Despite numerous policy initiatives and a large investment in the service, modernisation has not been fast enough to satisfy its desire to effect a transformational change in the service received by patients. The NHS is still orientated too much towards producers rather than consumers of care.

The 'top-down' centrist approach favoured since 1997 has had some effect. For example, there are now many more central institutions setting standards and measuring and inspecting performance, and staff on the ground in the NHS have clearly focused on achieving centrally-set targets – for example, reducing waiting times for inpatient treatment. Much is being asked of NHS staff, and many changes have been made, but key improvements for patients are either too slow (or, in a service as large as the NHS, not yet sufficiently visible at national level) to show that real progress has been made, despite the extra resources. Furthermore, achieving a key target – reducing waiting times for elective care – has proved to be slow, expensive and difficult.

The drive to improve performance

The Government is more urgently asking fundamental questions about how to effect change in order to improve performance in large public sector organisations such as the NHS. The discussion turns on the old political question of the extent to which monopoly state provision and financing can improve performance in the desired way, and how far sharper market incentives should be introduced. This discussion has featured in many key political speeches and papers – for example, the paper recently given by Chancellor Gordon Brown to the Social Market Foundation (Brown 2003). It has also been at the root of debate about recent policies – in particular, the proposal to introduce foundation trusts.

Policy directions

Despite the turbulence this is causing in policy circles, the reality is that the Government's business-as-usual instincts in terms of NHS policy are still firmly centrist in style. But, around the edges, there are three broad directions of policy aimed at improving performance in the NHS – in particular, making services more responsiveness to patients, which is the main policy priority. They are:

■ collaboration
■ devolution
■ enhancing market incentives.

These are described in detail below:

■ **Collaboration.** First, efforts have continued to encourage collaboration locally to encourage more integrated or seamless working across public services, to improve the care of users. Examples include the introduction of the statutory duty of partnership and long-term agreements between stakeholders in the local health and local government economy, and other policies that demand closer working – for example, in implementing the national service frameworks. This looks like 'centrally mandated' collaboration, but collaboration is the aim nonetheless.

■ **Devolution.** Second, there is a newer trend to devolve power locally in the NHS – for example, by giving more of the NHS budget directly to primary care trusts – and to encourage greater public involvement in the decisions of local health bodies – for example, through the stakeholder councils of the new foundation trusts, and through the local work of the Commission for Public and Patient Involvement. As the Secretary of State remarked in a recent seminar on the 'new localism' (Milburn 2003), the new central institutions set up since 1997 to set standards, inspect and regulate health care have allowed the Government to 'let go' and devolve more power locally.

At least three key policies signify this trend:

- allowing primary care trusts to control 75 per cent of the NHS budget directly
- the proposed introduction of foundation trusts (Department of Health 2002a)
- the revamping of the national and local apparatus to involve the public and patients more in decision making within the NHS (Department of Health 2003).

Much could be said of this trend to devolve power, but it is not the subject of this discussion paper. It is suffice to say that, while the NHS remains funded largely through central taxation and is accountable through the Secretary of State to Parliament, it remains to be seen how 'real' devolution can be in practice, how long it will last, and how effective the new efforts to involve the public in decision making will be.

- **Enhancing market incentives.** Finally, there is the issue of enhancing market incentives on the provider side. This has been done by:
    - allowing a diversity of private and not-for-profit providers to compete for NHS contracts for secondary care.
    - allowing more autonomy for foundation trusts (especially to raise capital funds on the private market)
    - allowing greater choice of provider for patients waiting more than six months for elective surgery
    - encouraging competition between providers.

Competition, in the NHS at least, is being encouraged on the basis of quality rather than price, since NHS providers must adhere to a national set of prices. A new system of financial flows supports and underpins these arrangements (Department of Health 2002b). In the proposed GP contract, it is clear that primary care trusts will be allowed to contract with a diversity of primary care providers (British Medical Association 2003). No competition is encouraged yet on the demand side – that is, between commissioners of NHS-funded care – and so far, the

Government has been firm that there will be no new changes to the method of funding NHS care.

Of these three trends, the most significant is this final one, because it represents the most radical departure from previous Labour policy, and it is central to current heated debates over the future direction of the NHS. We have been here before. In 1991, the 'internal market' was introduced between providers to stimulate competition and more responsiveness to patients or their agents (general practitioners). But the environment is different now. Competition will be based on quality not price, information systems are much improved, and the system of regulation of providers is tighter. Will the 'market' work better this time? Should it be tried again?

Can market forces work?

These questions are the subject of the two papers in this discussion paper, written by two senior economists in health care. Julian Le Grand argues that the Government is enhancing market incentives on the provider side in the NHS once again. Drawing on evidence from the 1991 reforms – and more recently, from elsewhere in the public sector – he argues that the 'new market' can work if we learn the lessons from the 1990s and pay attention to how to provide incentives to clinical staff – specifically to consultants.

In the second paper, Peter Smith argues that markets can introduce very 'raw' incentives that can produce adverse outcomes – in particular, alienating clinicians, on whom the NHS depends more than any other staff group. These papers were the subject of a breakfast discussion at the King's Fund in February 2003. The publication concludes with some reflections on the positions of Smith and Le Grand, and draws upon some of the points raised at the breakfast discussion.

The case for the internal market

The Government is in the throes of developing an internal market in heath care, with patient choice, financial flows following patient choice, PCT commissioning, foundation hospitals, cost and volume contracting (Department of Health 2002b, p 13, Lewis 2002). But there is a general perception that the internal market did not work very well last time it was tried – in the 1990s, under the Conservative governments of Margaret Thatcher and John Major. So what guarantee is there that it will work this time?

The internal market in the 1990s

The first point to make is that while the original internal market may not have delivered as much as its proponents hoped, it did not do too badly – especially when aspects of its performance are compared with what has happened since it was officially abolished. For instance, from 1991–92 to 1996–97, hospital efficiency (as measured by the growth of activity relative to that of resources) increased by 1.7 per cent per year on average. But from 1997–98 to 1999–2000, it fell by 1.6 per cent per year on average (Le Grand 2002). In particular, GP fundholding seems to have been particularly effective, with recent research suggesting that it reduced waiting times and referral rates alike (Dowling 1997, Gravelle *et al* 2002).

Still, it is undoubtedly true that the market experiment did not bring about the massive changes in behaviour of the key actors that might have been expected, or dramatic, demonstrable improvements in services. This was partly because of the absence of any effective entry or exit strategy for providers, the restrictions on competition resulting from this and from the continuance of powerful elements of central control (Le Grand *et al* 1998). Also, there were problems:

sizeable transactions costs, inequities brought about by the splitting of purchasing between health authorities and GP fundholders and – just possibly – a reduction in some aspects of quality (Propper *et al* 2002).

A different approach

So will this Government's version do better? One answer is to say it will, simply because it will be different. Unlike in the old market, there will be no (allegedly) ineffective price competition (Department of Health 2002b, p 13). This time, prices will be fixed and competition will depend only on quality. This should reduce transactions costs. There was no quality regulator in the previous market. However, there will be in the new one – the Commission for Health Care Audit and Inspection – as well as a host of other bodies concerned about various aspects of quality, such as the National Institute for Clinical Excellence and the Modernisation Agency.

Foundation hospitals will supposedly have more freedoms than the old trusts, although it is not always clear precisely what these will be, especially following the Treasury's insistence that their borrowing should count against the Department of Health's overall borrowing limits. Entry of new providers will be encouraged, including those owned by private and foreign companies. Finally, the purchaser will be different: no two-tier purchasing via the health authority or the GP fundholder, but the blend of the two kinds of purchaser that is the primary care trust.

Some of these differences will undoubtedly make the market work better. These include the increased freedoms for foundation hospitals – if they materialise – and increased competition from private sector and foreign competitors. For others, it is not so clear. Price competition is not necessarily damaging – indeed, its use in the old internal market fuelled some of the successes of GP fundholding. PCTs, on the other hand, look as if they are developing into weak health authorities – too large, too unwieldy and too unskilled to play the market properly – instead of becoming strong fundholders, as many of us hoped they would.

A comparison with primary education

A yet more fundamental problem concerns motivation and incentives. To examine this in more detail, it is useful to look at another area within the public sector, outside of health care, where a similar type of regulated internal or quasi-market has been tried, rather successfully: that of primary schools.

A combination of open enrolment, league tables and formula funding has meant that state primary schools have been subject to competitive pressures of the kind now being (re)developed for the NHS. The results have been striking. The percentage of pupils reaching a given level of achievement in the attainment tests introduced in 1995 in England has steadily increased, especially at the primary school end.

Some of the improvements have been remarkable. The percentage of pupils gaining the expected level of competence in maths at the end of primary school moved from 45 per cent in 1995 to 70 per cent in 2001. This should be set against the fact that the best available evidence suggests that there was no improvement in the maths skills of children in the early years of secondary school for 30 years before 1995 (Glennerster 2002).

Moreover, these improvements were not confined to good schools. In fact, the lowest performing schools in 1995 were the ones to show the greatest improvement by 2001. The same is true of schools ranked according to the wealth of the area. Over that period, schools in poor areas were catching up with schools from rich ones. Polarisation – the greatest worry of the critics of the use of market pressures in education (and indeed in health care) – does not, in fact, seem to have been a problem.

These statistics need to be treated with caution. There are many anecdotal stories of 'teaching to the test' – and, indeed, of outright fraud. And we cannot draw the unequivocal conclusion that, even if the improvements are real, they are all due to the impact of the regulated competitive market. Some undoubtedly arose from the introduction of the decidedly non-market device of a compulsory numeracy and literacy hour. Nonetheless, more micro-level research has suggested that competition has been an important factor in levering up standards (Bradley *et al* 2001).

If this kind of competition has worked for primary school education, are there reasons to think that it will not work equally effectively in health care? As we have seen, analyses of the relative lack of success of the earlier version of the NHS internal market drew attention to a number of factors that impeded its working, including a lack of appropriate incentives and the continuation of heavy-handed central control (Le Grand *et al* 1998).

However, the comparison with primary education brings out another factor: in a school, the relevant decision-makers are head teachers. Head teachers are largely motivated by a desire to preserve or improve the financial health of the institution. This is in part a self-interested motivation: a desire to keep their own job. But it also has a public service component. They believe that by improving the financial health of their institutions, they also benefit their pupils and staff. Moreover, head teachers have direct managerial control over their staff, with considerable freedom to hire, fire and promote. They also have considerable autonomy over pupil admissions and exclusions. Hence they have both the motivation and the ability to respond to market pressures.

Compare this with the situation facing those in charge of a hospital competing in the old internal market. Those nominally in charge of the institution were managers, motivated in large part by similar factors as head teachers: self-interest in the financial health of the institution, but also a public service concern for the quality of care. However, they had little direct managerial control over the key members of their staff who were providing that care – the consultants – and the consultants were largely a law unto themselves.

The consultants' perspectives

The consultants had considerable freedom of action in allocating resources. They, too, were motivated by a variety of considerations – not just self-interested ones concerning their own income and professional status, but also more altruistic motivations arising from their professional concern for patients. Crucially, though, they were not necessarily motivated by a concern for the financial health of the institution. Whatever happened to the hospital finances, they were very unlikely to lose their jobs or their incomes, and those with substantial incomes from private practice were even more secure. So they were not concerned with the impact of market pressures on the hospital, and those pressures had relatively little impact on them.

The problem for the Government's new version of the internal market in health care is that all of this is still true. The (old) consultant contract gives little personal incentive for consultants to increase their workload when overall resources increase, relying instead essentially on their good will and sense of commitment to their patients.

Indeed, many consultants face a perverse incentive structure when they are dealing with a patient with the means to pay privately. If the consultants arrange private treatment for their patient, the patient will be treated more quickly (thus benefiting the patient and meeting the consultant's professional concern) plus the consultant is paid, thus furthering his or her self-interest. On the other hand, if the consultant arranges for the patient to receive treatment under the NHS, the patient waits and the consultants gets an increase in his or her workload for no extra reward.

The consultant contract

The new consultant contract – now rejected by the consultants – attempted to deal with some of these problems. In return for a substantial pay increase, consultants were asked to commit more time to the NHS and less to private practice. There were to be positive incentives involving salary progression, with higher levels of pay depending on compliance with an agreed job plan, on meeting personal objectives and on evidence of no conflict of interest with private practice. In addition, during their first seven years, newly appointed consultants had either to undertake no private practice at all or, if they had a private practice, had first to offer eight extra hours to the NHS.

Would the new contract have worked? More specifically, would it have delivered higher consultant productivity within the NHS? It seems unlikely. It relied upon hospital managers being able to exercise a significant degree of control over consultants. Specifically, they would have had to evaluate consultants' job plans and assess whether they were meeting personal objectives, alongside the 'evidence' concerning potential conflicts of interest. If the evaluation revealed weaknesses in any of these respects, the managers concerned were to deny the consultant their pay progression.

But it is difficult to imagine them doing that effectively. Differences in expertise, status and power have meant that hospital managers have not been good at challenging consultants in the past. Since those fundamental differences have not changed, there seems little reason to suppose that they would have done better, even with the powers in the new contract.

Moreover, the perverse incentive with respect to private practice would have remained – for senior consultants, at least. In the absence of effective sanctions, it would still have been of direct benefit both to consultant and patient for the patient to have private treatment.

Luckily, the new contract has been rejected, and there is now an opportunity to change things more radically in order to deal with the incentive problems. But how? Here, the primary school model is of limited help. The success of the schools was partly derived from managerial power, and the failure of the contract has illustrated how difficult it is to increase managerial power, in a hospital context.

The fee-for-service option

An alternative is to move in the direction of a more market-oriented system of payment: fee-for-service. Consultants in the relevant specialities could be paid for providing extra services above a caseload baseline at, say, 80 per cent of the private sector rate for each unit of service provided. This would effectively remove the conflict of interest with private practice, since a consultant doing extra work in the public sector would still be getting four-fifths of what they could have earned in the private sector.

This would be a relatively small sacrifice, and one that most consultants would be compensated for by easier working conditions and the fact that they retain their commitment to NHS patients. There would be no need for managers to try to micro-manage consultants, as they would be doing what the managers and the Government wanted anyway. Consultants would have greater freedom of action, while managers would be spared unproductive confrontations.

Fee-for-service has many problems as a payment system. It can lead to too much treatment being provided, and outside the relatively simple cases of elective surgery, the 'service' being paid for can be difficult to define and measure. But the fact that other countries, such as the Netherlands, use it in their public and private sectors suggests that these difficulties are not insuperable. In any case, so long as the private sector retains fee-for-service, the public sector has little option but to follow suit. As long as consultants have the option of working in both sectors, the one offering a direct link between fees and extra work will always win.

Learning from the past

In short, the new market can work if the lessons from the old one, and from other areas of market operation in the public sector, are learned. One problem in particular needs to be addressed: the fact that the current payment system for consultants provides them with little incentive to respond to market pressures. It would seem that if markets are to work in health care, market principles have to be applied within the relevant institutions, as well as outside them.

The case against the internal market

The outcomes of any system of health care depend ultimately on the actions of frontline clinicians and their multifarious interactions with patients. The effectiveness of any set of institutional arrangements should be judged on the extent to which it nurtures or inhibits achievement of those outcomes. The key criterion for assessing the merits of increased provider competition should therefore, in my view, be its impact on the behaviour of health care professionals, and consequently on outcomes for patients. This paper sets out some of the potential perils associated with increased competition in health care.

The current situation

For the NHS, the point of departure is the existing set of institutional arrangements, which – although ostensibly repudiating the market – already contain some elements of competition. Many primary care commissioners do have some choice about where they send patients, so many providers have at least some incentive to attend to competitive pressures. A failure to capture sufficient business would at the very least expose a provider's management to awkward questions about its performance.

However, the ultimate sanctions and rewards of a true market – for example, in the form of bankruptcy and closure – do not, in general, apply. Equally, the NHS does not allow retention of provider surpluses, so a key market incentive for technological innovations and cost savings is absent. The question to be addressed is therefore not whether or not a market should be introduced. It is rather whether NHS outcomes would be improved by sharper market incentives than at present exist – for example, in the form of real risk of organisational failure and retention of surpluses.

This section seeks in very broad terms to identify the main impact on clinical actions of the introduction of increased competitive forces into the NHS. It is written in the light of proposals for the NHS to revise provider funding by reimbursing providers according to national healthcare resource group (HRG) costs (Department of Health 2002b). In effect, a provider's revenue will, in future, be determined, at least in part, by the volume of activity it attracts. However, it is important to note that the market incentives apparently implicit in this arrangement will be, to some extent, diluted if they are not accompanied by regulatory reforms, in the form of:

- bankruptcy threat
- freedom from capital controls
- power to retain surpluses.

It will be interesting to see whether the proposed parallel reforms to the ownership status of NHS hospitals will introduce some or all of these reforms (Department of Health 2002a).

Benefits of competition

Competitive provider markets have obvious attractions for health care policy makers. Markets stimulate providers to maximise long–run profits, and conventional economic theory suggests that, given a satisfactory regulatory framework, they will have a number effects, including to:

- encourage managerial efficiency
- stimulate the entry of new providers when supply is inadequate
- lead to efficient contraction in capacity when supply is in surplus
- promote quality improvements and innovation
- reduce production costs.

Furthermore, decisions about the closure and reconfiguration of providers will be delegated to 'the market', absolving policy-makers of direct responsibility for what are often highly contentious changes.

Dangers of competition

The policy intention is therefore that profits should be pursued through cost reduction, technological innovation and quality improvement. However, in health care many other considerations could contribute to profits, such as:

- securing monopoly power over provision
- withholding or distorting information about outputs and outcomes
- maintaining secrecy about clinical practices in order to retain competitive advantage
- discouraging treatment of relatively high-cost or high-risk patients who should benefit from treatment
- encouraging treatment of relatively low-cost or low-risk patients for whom treatment may not be justified.

Payment mechanisms

Central to the operation of a health care market is the payment mechanism for clinical activity. This acts as the fundamental market incentive, and provider organisations can therefore be expected to respond very directly to it. Typically, payment for reasonably discrete health care interventions, such as elective surgery, will be in the form of either:

- a lump sum, regardless of output (block contract)
- a fixed price per case.

These are likely to encourage, respectively:

- deterrence of patients seeking the intervention
- encouragement of patients (at least low-risk patients for whom the price exceeds the expected cost – so-called 'cream skimming').

Of course, intermediate payment mechanisms are possible, yielding intermediate incentives for providers.

Some experiments such as the 'Rewarding Results' initiative in the United States (National Health Care Purchasing Institute 2002) are beginning to reward providers on the basis of outcomes as well as activity. However, these are at a very early stage of development, and the reality is that almost all financial payments in health care markets are linked only to the volume of clinical activity. So, crudely put, the market incentives are either to minimise throughput (under block contracts), or to maximise profitable throughput (under price per case), without direct consideration of quality. Under either form of contract, therefore, providers have an incentive to skimp on aspects of treatment for which no direct fee is received – in particular, clinical quality.

Promoting quality

There is a line of thought that there is a 'business case for quality' that obviates the need to worry unduly about the potential for skimping (Institute of Medicine 2001). Certainly, careful attention to some aspects of clinical quality – such as hospital-acquired infection – may reduce the provider's expected costs, and therefore contribute to long-run profits. However, the benefits of many other quality issues may benefit either the individual (a longer, healthier life) or other agencies (less social care needed) rather than the health care provider.

An alternative approach to addressing quality is to empower patients to demand high-quality care. In the past, such empowerment was generally infeasible, given the overwhelming informational advantages of doctors. However, the growth of an increasingly informed and assertive citizenry, bolstered by instruments such as the National Service Frameworks, may help empower some types of patients – in particular, the 'expert' patient with a chronic condition (Department of Health 2001). It is difficult to argue against such developments. But it is important to note that a reliance on empowerment may allow the empowered to secure better health care at the expense of those unwilling or unable to challenge clinical decisions. In short, it is quite conceivable that a reliance on markets will lead to increased disparities in access and outcomes, so key equity objectives may be compromised.

Another way of promoting quality is to publish measures of the clinical outcome secured by a provider. Publication of such performance data has much to commend it, most notably because within a market setting it does appear to motivate providers to examine their own performance (Marshall *et al* 2000). However, there is little evidence that patients or their general practitioners take any notice of performance measures. Moreover, the science of outcome measurement is in its infancy, and most aspects of health care will remain resistant to reliable and meaningful outcome measurement for the foreseeable future. So an important requirement for a properly functioning market – informed purchasers – may be absent.

Stimulating unwarranted demand

Finally, assuming a price-per-case regime, there is considerable scope for providers to stimulate unwarranted demand for health care when patients are insured, and therefore do not bear the direct costs of treatment (McGuire 2000). Such 'physician-induced demand' has been a particular preoccupation in the market-based (and manifestly dysfunctional) US health care market. It is associated with free entry to provider markets, and can lead to what would generally be seen as excess supply of medical services. It may seem that – at least in the short term – incentives to increase the supply of medical personnel may be a beneficial by-product of introducing competitive forces into the UK. Yet the implication is that without vigorous performance management, the increased supply might be channelled into providing unnecessary or low-priority health care.

Inequality in care

When consideration moves beyond the acute sector towards more complex aspects of health care, such as the management of chronic conditions, the limitations of the market incentives become even more apparent. Purchasers may be able to design incentives to undertake interventions that are unambiguously associated with good outcomes (such as regular blood-glucose and blood-pressure measurement for diabetic patients). However, these will have to be discrete activities that cannot possibly capture the whole spectrum of integrated care required by such patients. Instead, providers will have ample scope to skimp on quality, or shift the costs of care onto the individual or other agencies.

Furthermore, the variations in cost for patients within a given chronic category are, in general, very large compared with those within acute categories, and providers can readily seek out information on chronic patients to determine at which end of the cost spectrum they lie. In short, the scope for gains from 'cream skimming' and quality skimping are particularly large in the chronic sector. An unfettered market is therefore likely to have especially adverse outcomes for chronic care.

In short, it can quite plausibly be argued that as well as generating intended benefits, such as growth in activity, increased use of markets might lead to seriously adverse outcomes, in the form of:

■ reductions in clinical quality
■ discrimination against relatively sick patients
■ heightened inequalities.

Previous competition in the NHS

It might be argued that the NHS has tried employing market forces before, and providers did not appear to respond so directly to the market incentives (Le Grand *et al* 1998). However, the NHS internal market never operated as a 'true' market – in particular, few providers were allowed to fail, and they were not able to retain surpluses. And there is increasing evidence that, even with the attenuated incentives that did operate, providers did indeed respond as expected. For example, there was an increase in the measured volume of hospital activity, and fundholding GPs secured a marked reduction in referrals for elective procedures relative to their non-fundholding counterparts (Dusheiko *et al* 2002).

Furthermore, there is evidence that heightened competition may have led to a serious deterioration in clinical outcomes (Propper *et al* 2002) and that purchasers with market power (fundholders) could secure lower waiting times than others. These outcomes demonstrate that agents do respond to incentives, even in a very diluted form of market. How much greater might the responses – both intended and adverse – be in a purer market framework?

Reimbursement mechanisms

Economists have explored in some depth reimbursement mechanisms that might correct at least some of the adverse outcomes of pure price-per-case payment. One of the clearest and most consistent findings emerging from the US literature is that a health care resource group (HRG) system of payment should be accompanied by some 'cost sharing' (Dranove and Satterthwaite 2000). That is, the provider should be reimbursed for some of the additional costs of expensive patients, over and above the HRG payment. There are, of course, numerous practical impediments to such an arrangement, but the

message from US researchers is that some adverse outcomes from
market systems can be tempered with judicious adjustments to crude
contractual arrangements.

There are also serious checks on the worst excesses of an uninhibited
market outcome in health care. These arise, in the words of Kenneth
Arrow (one of the most distinguished of economists), because:

> ... when the market fails to achieve an optimal state, society will, to
> some extent at least, recognize the gap, and nonmarket social
> institutions will arise attempting to bridge it

Arrow (1963), pp 941–73

Professional ethic

In health care, the most celebrated of these non-market institutions are
the health care professions. These serve numerous purposes, but one
of the most important is to transmit an ethic or culture to professionals
that is intended to transcend immediate contractual incentives. When
outcomes are difficult to measure and the production process complex,
we can rely on neither markets (because contracts will necessarily be
incomplete) nor bureaucracies (because rules of behaviour cannot be
codified). Instead, we must rely on professional codes to guide the
actions of clinicians (Fuchs 1996).

The professional ethic is fundamental to health care because contracts
between purchaser and provider can never be remotely complete.
Indeed, we have shown that they are likely, in practice, to be very crude,
with payments usually being based on case-mix-adjusted activity.
The role of professional culture in these circumstances should be to
guide the actions of clinicians towards preferred behaviour, even when
there is no direct instruction or incentive to comply. Professional norms
play a crucial role in ameliorating the inevitable imperfections in
market contracts.

Unfortunately, we do not yet have a convincing model of the clinical professional's motivations and preferences, and how they affect the clinical outcomes secured for patients. However, it is likely that three key factors combine to influence the effectiveness of the clinician and the team within which he or she works:

■ the information made available to them
■ personal incentives
■ professional culture.

Information systems

In principle, one of the major benefits of a unitary health care system such as the NHS is the opportunity it offers to standardise information systems. The NHS Plan envisages an electronic health record for all citizens, available for access by all NHS providers by 2005 (Department of Health 2000). The core function of the clinical information system is to provide for patients and staff a 'real-time' resource that is an essential element in the delivery of high-quality patient care. A well-designed electronic information system would serve two core performance purposes:

■ to prompt clinicians to deliver appropriate interventions, in line with clinical guidelines
■ to check that such interventions have been delivered.

Good-quality performance information for benchmarking purposes, at any desired level of aggregation, will then be a natural by-product of the information base.

In practice, the NHS has a lamentable history of piecemeal, poor-quality and failed information systems. This may be mainly due to a historical lack of political commitment – a situation that has now (happily) been reversed. Developments in this area have the potential to secure a far more immediate and direct impact on physician behaviour than the introduction of competitive forces.

Personal performance incentives

Personal incentives can be designed or accidental. To date, the NHS has traditionally paid little attention to designed personal incentives, and the way in which organisational incentives (in the form of performance ratings or market forces) filter down to frontline staff is haphazard or non-existent. Reliance on informal incentives (such as professional prestige, career advancement and intrinsic satisfaction in good performance) may, in some circumstances, be perfectly satisfactory.

However, Mannion and Goddard (2001) found little evidence of any impact on clinical practice of publishing clinical outcomes data for Scottish hospitals. They attribute this to a number of causes, including a lack of incentives to scrutinise and act on the data. That is, the accidental incentives were not, on their own, strong enough to induce clinical responses on any material scale. It is an open question whether the proposed changes to clinical terms of employment will give NHS managers enough flexibility to put in place incentives appropriate to each clinical situation. However, it is, in my view, this aspect of personal incentives – rather than the crude profit-maximising incentives embedded in the market – to which policy-makers should be paying most attention.

Economists traditionally focus on information and incentives as the main devices to secure performance improvement. Yet there is a third determinant of behaviour long recognised by sociologists: the intrinsic objectives of personnel. In the extreme, if these are identical to the objectives society holds for its health care system, then there should be no need for incentives. Society could rely on professionals to work exactly as intended. In practice, of course, there is an imperfect correspondence between the objectives of 'principal' (citizens or patients) and 'agent' (clinician). But is that disjunction immutable. Or can system design and managerial action bring clinical objectives closer to those of society? In the language I used earlier, can the NHS affect professional culture?

The Bristol Inquiry report argued that failures in the organisational culture – embracing attitudes towards safety, accountability, openness and teamwork – were crucial to the tragic outcomes at Bristol, and proposed a 'cultural transformation' of the NHS (Bristol Royal Infirmary Inquiry 2001). Among other things, organisational culture reflects the values and beliefs underlying the actions of personnel. It is almost certainly the case that the success of performance improvement efforts will be highly dependent on the cultural environment – affecting, for example, the readiness of staff to cross traditional professional boundaries. But how a favourable culture can be encouraged and nurtured remains a largely unresolved issue (Davies *et al* 2000).

Professional networks

There are, nevertheless, signs that the NHS is waking up to the fundamental importance of professional culture. The natural way for the clinician to assess his or her own performance is with reference to others in the same discipline. This interest in the actions and performance of professional peers can be exploited in powerful ways, through the medium of the professional networks and collaboratives that are now emerging. These include the intensive care case-mix programme, the risk-stratified data on cardiac surgery outcomes at a national level, and the numerous local initiatives, most notably in cancer care (Rowan and Black 2000; Keogh and Kinsman 1999).

The essence of these networks should be that they are clinically led (by professionals of all relevant disciplines) and focus on the needs of patients rather than organisations. They should offer timely and relevant benchmarking information for peer review, tailored specifically to the speciality under scrutiny. Networks require professional leadership and support in the form of system development and investment of time and money. At their best, such mechanisms should offer an incentive for all professionals to:

- improve continuously their own performance
- seek out best practice
- expose unacceptable performance.

The key challenge to nurturing the development of successful networks is to integrate the top-down managerial imperatives (whether market competition or performance management) with a system of clinical networks. These should reflect a professional concern with:

- clinical quality
- patient focus
- peer review
- continuous improvement.

In this respect, the role of senior managers is crucial. One of their core clinical governance responsibilities should be to nurture effective clinical networks. This cannot be the only element of clinical governance. A minority of clinicians will not participate, or will even seek to subvert, performance management. There remains a problem of how to remedy poor performance once it is identified. Moreover, some specialities may lack the leadership or will to go down this route. And for all clinical areas, there will be a need for external support and advice on good practice – a natural role for the Modernisation Agency. However, effective clinical networks should be an indispensable element of clinical governance and, by implication, successful health outcomes.

Again, it is difficult to see how the introduction of a competitive market will help the move towards a more effective professional culture. Indeed, it is tempting to argue that the competitive culture is antipathetic to the desirable features of professional behaviour outlined above. There is considerable evidence that the preferences of public service employees are, to some extent, formed by the system in which they are asked to work (Le Grand 1997), and it is quite plausible to argue that the encouragement of competitive behaviour will adversely affect professional willingness to share experience and undertake activities that lie outside contractual requirements.

Conclusions

There are, therefore, some distinct perils associated with a move towards increased competition in the NHS. These perils are likely to be relatively immaterial for some acute aspects of care with homogenous patient groups, for which there are good measures of outcome and well-understood technologies. Competition undoubtedly confers many benefits alongside the perils that I have sketched out above, and so, at the very least, it seems sensible to experiment carefully with the introduction of sharper competitive pressures for such interventions.

Yet even such modest experimentation runs the risk of focusing managers' attention on the competitive sector, at the expense of the non-acute sector. It is difficult to envisage circumstances in which a truly competitive market can be created for many common (and costly) chronic conditions with heterogeneous patient groups, for which there are:

- few – if any – measures of outcome
- complex patient pathways
- highly contingent approaches to treatment
- high reliance on interactions with other agencies, such as social care.

Here, the emphasis should, in my view, be on the development of information bases, designing appropriate incentives into terms of employment, and nurturing a professional culture of sharing experience and seeking out continuous improvement. For all its weaknesses, the current performance management regime, rather than competition, would seem to offer the best prospect for securing improvements in this sphere (Smith 2002). Competition will, at best, merely distract managers from the central task of securing the most cost-effective care for such patients.

In short, true market competition introduces a set of very raw incentives that carry serious potential for adverse outcomes for many aspects of health care. The outcomes of any system of health care depend ultimately on the actions of frontline clinicians, and careful attention needs to be given to the impact of competition on professional behaviour. If these are not addressed, the costs of market reforms are likely to greatly outweigh any benefits they generate.

Ways ahead

Discussion about introducing stronger market incentives on the provider side in the NHS seems 'academic' in one main respect: there is a shortage of supply in the UK in the form of staff and buildings. While the NHS Plan sets out how the supply of staff will be increased, according to current trends it is likely to take five to ten years (Gray, Finlayson 2002). On this basis, it is unlikely that meaningful competition – and, probably, choice – among providers will be possible for at least five years. However, it is important to debate now whether stronger market incentives are desirable because in the next five years, in the absence of ideal conditions for a market, there will be considerable room for experimentation and evaluation.

In one sense, the positions of Le Grand and Smith are quite different. Le Grand believes that greater patient choice coupled with competition between providers (hospitals) is worth trying again. Smith is far less sanguine, even about modest experimentation with market incentives. Yet in one key respect the authors agree: both believe that the motivation of clinicians is a key consideration if the introduction of sharper market incentives is to be pursued by policy-makers. Le Grand suggests that stronger financial incentives should be used to prompt clinicians (in particular, consultants) to be more productive; Smith worries especially about the possible detrimental effect of these, and other market-based incentives, on motivation. This terrain is explored briefly below.

Should an internal market be tried again?

Both authors refer to the evidence of the impact of the 1991 reforms, which introduced stronger market incentives into the NHS. They agree that the overall balance sheet was mixed, for example:

- increased productivity by secondary care providers
- a possible decrease in quality of care in hospitals
- a reduction in referrals to hospital by GP fundholders
- increased transactions costs
- some inequity of access to services of patients of non-fundholding compared to fundholding practices.

Both also agree that the incentives produced by the 1991 reforms were weak, and that the internal market did not operate as a true market. After this point, the two authors differ. Le Grand suggests that market incentives could now be stronger, especially as there are now new structures (such as the new system of national standards, regulation and measures of performance) that could help to spot and curtail undesirable consequences. Smith, however, argues that despite these new structures, a key check on the adverse effects of stronger market incentives is the professional ethic, which could be seriously undermined (as argued below), resulting in poorer care and clinical outcomes for patients.

In discussions of the potential effects of market incentives on hospitals, it is often assumed that hospitals provide a homogenous set of services. But, as Smith goes on to note, there are important differences between elective care (non-urgent surgery) and the care of people (often older people) with chronic diseases. Elective care is generally uncomplicated and predictable. For these reasons, it is an area in which there is already a private market, which has proved to be successful – certainly as far as patients, clinicians, and indeed the NHS (the largest provider of privately funded care in the UK) are concerned – although escalating costs, reflected in higher premiums, have been a problem.

However, the costliest conditions to treat in the NHS are not these quick and easy elective procedures, but complex, chronic medical conditions. A recent paper in Health Affairs listed the costliest conditions in the USA: chronic conditions such as asthma, diabetes and chronic congestive heart failure were far costlier than conditions requiring elective procedures (Druss *et al* 2002).

Care for patients with these conditions requires care across an integrated care pathway – much of it upstream in primary care. The philosophy regarding hospital care may be different to elective care – admission to hospital for chronic medical conditions is considered a sign of failure rather than success. Care requires longstanding relations between professionals and the patient, working together, and incentives would need to be designed to reflect this. This type of care, then, may require:

- some capitated envelope of funding
- provision along an integrated care model
- development of longstanding relationships between clinicians across institutions who know the patient well
- incentives aligned to encourage this to happen.

As Smith argues, a competitive market between providers, or groups of clinicians, might weaken the professional culture that seeks to put patient care first, thus reducing the collaboration between clinicians that is necessary to provide good care.

Motivating clinicians

On the motivation of clinicians, Le Grand argues that it may be desirable to pay consultants on a fee-for-service basis to provide incentives for greater productivity. Smith argues that there will be detrimental effects from a contestable market among hospitals – that is, a situation that allows for some if not all forms of market discipline – on clinicians' motivation. In particular it is likely to affect altruism and other professional values that help clinicians put patients' interest above other considerations. In fact, both may well be true, and a first step forward must be to work towards strengthening professional values, going beyond the useful efforts that the General Medical Council has pursued in recent years. This will be important, however the health care system is structured and financed in future, since clinicians will face increasing pressure from the state to manage resources more effectively.

Le Grand points to the important role taken by head teachers in primary schools, and how market incentives combined with greater autonomy and managerial control over resources (he does not make clear which) have resulted in strikingly positive effects. He also contrasts this state of affairs with the position of the consultants who, in the main, do not exercise much managerial control within hospitals at a strategic level, and whose objectives may be quite different to hospital managers who do.

A recent edition of the *British Medical Journal* (22 March 2003) and the *Health Services Journal* (27 March 2003) highlighted these differences, and how they can lead to either indifference of the clinicians towards strategic goals set by management or, worse, conflict. If market incentives for hospitals were made stronger, then, unless more work were done to encourage clinicians to engage in strategic management, consultants might be indifferent to such incentives, and the differences in objectives between clinicians and managers might increase. That may be why Le Grand focuses on the importance of considering incentives directly for consultants, rather than just for institutions.

Two examples here may be instructive of how the objectives of hospital clinicians might be better aligned with management. The first is the experience of the professional executive committee (PEC) in primary care trusts – committees entirely made up of clinicians who advise the board on operational and clinical matters, and who have considerable power and influence. Since the PECs have been operating for a short time, it will be important to evaluate their benefit. The second is the interesting arrangement that exists in Kaiser Permanente, a US-managed care organisation whose organisational values, mission and structure resembles the NHS in many respects (Feachem *et al* 2002). The strategic goals of Kaiser Permanente are agreed upon, and worked towards, by three groups:

■ those representing the 'Plan' (the insurance arm of the organisation)
■ the hospitals owned by Kaiser
■ the 'Permanente Medical Group' – all the medically qualified clinicians working in Kaiser.

As a result there is significant 'buy-in' from the medical staff.

Conclusion

If we agree that a 'one size fits all' model is inappropriate for a modern NHS, then a 'one size fits all' market for secondary care providers, fitting all types of care, is also likely to be inappropriate. The implication is that two tracks may now be open for health policy: encouragement by Government for a more contestable market on the provider side for elective care, and a different approach for chronic disease as noted above.

Alternatively, it may be that the Government's current vision of a 'market' in the NHS harks back too much to the 1991 split between purchasers (health authorities and fundholders) and secondary care providers. New and stronger market incentives could be radically different to those introduced then. For example, incentives could encourage a contestable market between more vertically integrated providers (for example, between primary and secondary care located in one organisation), specifically to improve the quality of chronic care. Foundation status could be allowed for whole health economies of providers, or networks of clinicians, with competition for contracts from commissioners and, in future, competition for patients between commissioners.

Lessons here could come from the USA, where there has been a good deal of work to identify the main elements of chronic disease management, and how incentives might better be aligned and care organised to improve quality (Wagner *et al* 1996, 1999) . However, this is a system in which there is fierce competition between insurers (for enrolees) and providers of care (for contracts), and a high level of pressure from consumers, unlike the UK. A major King's Fund project is underway in 2003 to identify key lessons for the UK from leading managed care organisations specifically in managing chronic diseases in a market environment.

In the medium term, at least two things are clear. First, a contestable market of providers, coupled with greater choice of provider for patients, will be encouraged in the NHS over the next few years. At a King's Fund breakfast debate on the subject ('Can market forces be used for good?' 26 February 2003), the majority of participants among an audience of senior policy-makers and managers were in favour of this direction of policy.

Second, the health care environment will not be 'tranquil', but dynamic and changeable, as new opportunities arise, both from the external environment and from new policies. The pace and scope of change is likely to be dominated in the short term by two events: the ability of the NHS to achieve the targets set out in the NHS Plan, and the next general election. If Labour is re-elected, and the NHS is not perceived to be changing fast enough, then pressure will grow to introduce stronger market incentives on the demand side.

Ways forward

The role of market forces in a modern NHS is one of a range of important, inter-linked issues shaping the future of our health service that need further research and analysis if decisions are to be based on sound evidence. The King's Fund will continue to contribute to wider debate, through research and publishing activities, and by hosting a series of expert debates. Our Shaping the New NHS programme will explore a number of key strands:

- **The impacts of new forms of competition and choice.** We will research the impacts of the new fixed-price market in the NHS, looking at the implications and likely results of new financial flows, of allowing non-NHS providers to contract for NHS care, and of enhancing patient choice. In collaboration with a number of other organisations and academics, we will contribute to an evaluation of the London Patients' Choice Project.

- **Choice and equity.** We will explore how best to balance the interests of the individual consumer and the public as a whole in efforts to improve the quality of patient care, hosting an expert seminar in September 2003 and publicising the results.

- **The role of market forces in primary care.** We will examine whether stronger market incentives should be applied in primary care providers and primary care trusts – and, if so, how.

■ **The role of an 'arms-length' NHS agency.** We will look at the case for and against continued direct management of the NHS by the Department of Health, and the feasibility of a new semi-independent health service.

■ **The role of medical professionalism.** We will research how professionals might best be supported in order to respond to new challenges, such as stronger market incentives.

■ **The management of chronic care.** We will research how stronger market forces might best be applied to enhance the management of patients with multiple and chronic medical conditions, drawing on lessons learned from managed care organisations in the United States.

■ **Decentralisation and the 'new localism'.** We will analyse whether attempts by Government to decentralise power in the NHS, and to give the public more power in shaping health services locally, will improve provider responsiveness in ways that obviate the need for stronger market incentives.

■ **The role of information in health and health care.** We are exploring the role and impact of increasing information in health and health care, through a series of workshops with users and providers of health services.

See *Linked publications: forthcoming titles* (pages 44–49) for details of proposed published outputs and dates.

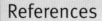

References

Arrow K (1963). 'Uncertainty and the welfare economics of medical care'. *American Economic Review*, vol 53(5), pp 941–73.

Bradley S, Johnes G, Millington J (2001). 'School choice, competition and the efficiency of secondary schools in England'. *European Journal of Operational Research*, vol 135, pp 545–68.

British Medical Association (2003). *Investing in General Practice: the new general medical services contract.* London: BMA. Available at: www.bma.org.uk/ap.nsf/Content/investinggp

Bristol Royal Infirmary Inquiry (2001). *Learning from Bristol: The report of the public enquiry into children's heart surgery at the Bristol Royal Infirmary 1984–1995.* London: The Stationery Office.

Brown G (2003). *A modern agenda for prosperity and social reform.* Speech made by the Chancellor of the Exchequer, Gordon Brown, to the Social Market Foundation at the Cass Business School, London, 3 February 2003. Available at: www.hm-treasury.gov.uk/newsroom_and_speeches/press/2003/ press_12_03.cfm

Davies H, Nutley S, Mannion R (2000). 'Organisational culture and quality of health care'. *Quality in Health Care*, vol 9, pp 111–19.

Department of Health (2000). *The NHS Plan: A plan for investment, a plan for reform.* London: The Stationery Office.

Department of Health (2001). *The Expert Patient: A new approach to chronic disease management for the 21st century.* London: Department of Health.

Department of Health (2002a). *NHS Foundation Trusts: Eligibility criteria and timetable*. London: Department of Health.

Department of Health (2002b). *Reforming NHS Financial Flows: Introducing payment by results*. London: Department of Health.

Department of Health (2003). *Strengthening accountability: involving patients and the public: practice guidance, Section 11 of the Health and Social Care Act 2001*. London: Department of Health.

Dowling B (1997). 'The effect of fundholding on waiting times: database study'. *British Medical Journal*, vol 315, pp 290–92.

Dranove D, Satterthwaite M (2000). 'The industrial organisation of health care markets', in Newhouse JP, Culyer AJ (eds) *Handbook of Health Economics*. Amsterdam: Elsevier.

Druss BG, Marcus SC, Olfson M, Pincus HA (2002). 'The most expensive medical conditions in America'. Health Affairs, vol 21, pp 105–11.

Dusheiko M, Gravelle H, Jacobs R, Smith P (2002). *The Effect of Budgets on Doctor Behaviour: Evidence from a natural experiment*. York: Centre for Health Economics, University of York.

Feachem RGA, Sekhri NK, White KL (2002). 'Getting more for their dollar: a comparison of the NHS with California's Kaiser Permanente'. *British Medical Journal*, vol 324, pp 135–43.

Fuchs V (1996). 'Economics, values, and health care reform'. *American Economic Review*, vol 86(1), pp 1–24.

Glennerster H (2002). 'United Kingdom Education 1997–2001'. *Oxford Review of Economic Policy*, vol 18, pp 120–36.

Gravelle H, Dusheiko M, Sutton M (2002). 'The demand for elective surgery in a public system: time and money prices in the UK national health services'. *Journal of Health Economics,* vol 21, pp 357–531.

Gray D, Finlayson B (2002). 'Strong Medicine'. *The Guardian,* 8 Oct 2002.

Institute of Medicine (2001). *Crossing the Quality Chasm: A new health system for the 21st century.* Washington: National Academy Press.

Keogh B, Kinsman R (1999). *National Adult Cardiac Surgical Database Report, 1998.* London: The Society of Cardiothoracic Surgeons of Great Britain and Ireland.

Le Grand J (1997). 'Knights, knaves or pawns? Human behaviour and social policy'. *Journal of Social Policy,* vol 26(2), pp 149–69.

Le Grand, J (2002). 'The Labour Government and the NHS'. *Oxford Review of Economic Policy,* vol 18.

Le Grand J, Mays N, Mulligan J (eds) (1998). *Learning from the NHS Internal Market.* London: Kings Fund.

Lewis R (2002). 'Uh...haven't we been here before?'. *Health Matters,* (Autumn) No. 49.

McGuire T (2000). 'Physician agency', in Newhouse JP and Culyer AJ (eds.) *Handbook of Health Economics.* Amsterdam: Elsevier.

Mannion R, Goddard M (2001). 'Impact of published clinical outcomes data: case study in NHS hospital trusts'. *British Medical Journal,* vol 323, pp 260–63.

Marshall M, Shekelle P, Leatherman S, Brook R (2000). 'The public release of performance data: what do we expect to gain? A review of the literature'. *Journal of the American Medical Association,* vol 283, pp 1866–74.

Milburn A (2003). *Localism: From rhetoric to reality.* Lecture given by Secretary of State for Health, the Rt Hon Alan Milburn MP, 5 February 2003. Available at: www.nlgn.org.uk/nlgn.phppublic. London: Department of Health.

National Health Care Purchasing Institute (2002). *Ensuring Quality Providers: A purchaser's toolkit for using incentives.* Washington DC: National Health Care Purchasing Institute.

Propper C, Burgess S, Abraham D (2002). *Competition and Quality: Evidence from the NHS internal market 1991–1999.* Bristol: CMPO, University of Bristol.

Propper C, Burgess S, Green K (2002). 'Does competition between hospitals improve the quality of care? Hospital death rates and the NHS internal market'. Unpublished.

Rowan K, Black N (2000). 'A bottom-up approach to performance indicators through clinician networks'. *Health Care UK,* Spring 2000, pp 42–6.

Smith P (2002). 'Performance management in British health care: will it deliver?'. *Health Affairs,* vol 21(3), pp 103–15.

Wagner EH, Austin BT, Von Korff (1996). 'Organizing care for patients with chronic illness'. *Managed Care Quarterly,* vol 4; 2, pp 12–25.

Wagner EH, Davis C, Schaefer M, Von Korff, Austin B (1999). 'A survey of leading chronic disease management programs: are they consistent with the literature?'. *Managed Care Quarterly,* vol 7; 3, pp 56–66.

Linked publications

We publish a wide range of titles about the NHS. See below for a selection of published and forthcoming titles. For the full range of current titles, visit our online bookshop at www.kingsfund.org.uk/e-bookshop or call our bookshop on 020 7307 2591.

PUBLISHED TITLES

Future Directions for Primary Care Trusts
Jennifer Dixon, Stephen Gillam, Richard Lewis

Primary care trusts (PCTs) are at the sharp end of the Government's hopes for a modernised NHS that is more responsive to patients and built on new models of social ownership. This web paper analyses their new role and asks how they might develop in the future. It constructs three possible scenarios for debate: one that puts the consumer in the driving seat and makes maximum use of competition; another that puts equity first and makes minimal use of market forces; and an 'ethical market' that uses competition selectively where it is consistent with PCTs' wider social mission.

8 May 2003 Free
Download at www.kingsfund.org.uk

Sustaining Reductions in Waiting Times: Identifying successful strategies
John Appleby et al

Some trusts have been consistently successful in achieving – and in some cases, exceeding – the Government's inpatient waiting-time target of under six months. This web paper identifies the critical factors that have led to their success and analyses the context, including

managerial and operational characteristics that might be transferable
to other organisations.

May 2003 52pp Free
Download at www.kingsfund.org.uk/pdf/waitingtimes.pdf

Claiming The Health Dividend: Unlocking the benefits of NHS spending
Anna Coote

The NHS is more than a provider of health services – it is the largest
single organisation in the UK. How it recruits staff, procures food
or constructs buildings affects the wider social, economic and
environmental fabric of which it is part – which in turn affects people's
health. This major report opens up an important debate about how
the NHS might put its corporate muscle and spending power to work
for health improvement and sustainable development – and in doing
so ensure it promotes health, as well as offering health care.

ISBN 185717 464 X May 2002 150pp £10.00
Download a free report summary at www.kingsfund.org.uk/eKingsfund/
assets/applets/Claiming_the_Health_Dividend_summary.pdf

Five-Year Health Check: A review of government health policy 1997–2002
Anna Coote and John Appleby (eds)

When the Labour Government came to power in May 1997, it promised to
'save the NHS' by cutting waiting lists, improving service quality, raising
spending and reducing health inequalities. Five years on, this
comprehensive report scrutinises progress against pledges made by
the Government during its first term of office in areas such as funding,
staffing and quality of care. It argues that money alone, while crucial, will
not build a new NHS, and that professional, motivated staff and
a focus on wider health issues also have a key role to play.

ISBN 185717 463 1 April 2002 138pp £7.99

The Future of the NHS: A framework for debate

Should the Government be responsible for every 'dropped bedpan', or is it time for a decisive separation of political and managerial responsibilities? How can local responsiveness and innovation be supported alongside the drive for national standards? And can the extension of patient choice lever up quality? This paper, which brings together ideas from a group of commentators, academics and practitioners from health care and beyond, chaired by Lord Haskins, aims to stimulate the wider debate on which a reasoned, pragmatic consensus for the future depends.

Jan 2002 30pp Free
Download at
www.kingsfund.org.uk/eKingsfund/assets/applets/future_of_NHS.pdf

What Has New Labour Done for Primary Care? A balance sheet
Edited by Stephen Gillam. Foreword by Rudolf Klein

New Labour's first term in office saw a proliferation of new initiatives for the NHS. In primary care, these included significant changes in the form of the NHS Direct and walk-in health centres. This publication analyses the actual and potential impacts of these developments, and seeks to put them into the wider context of other changes in the NHS.

ISBN 185717 445 3 2001 128pp £7.99

The NHS – Facing the Future
Anthony Harrison and Jennifer Dixon

The NHS is under more pressure than ever before – from the public, the politicians and the media. This publication offers a wide-ranging examination of the modern health service, including new technology, an ageing population and rising consumer expectations. It argues that if the NHS is to survive in this new, more demanding environment, then standing still is not an option.

ISBN 185717 219 1 2000 342pp £17.99

The Politics of NHS Reform 1988-97: Metaphor or reality?
Chris Ham

How do the politicians closely involved with health and health care see the drive to reform the NHS that characterised the 1990s? Based on interviews with health secretaries who served between 1988–1997 – Kenneth Clarke, William Waldegrave, Virginia Bottomley and Stephen Dorrell – this publication probes their role and perceptions of what constituted a major experiment with internal markets.

ISBN 185717 417 8 2000 78pp £14.99

From Cradle to Grave
Geoffrey Rivett

Published to mark the NHS's 50th anniversary, this publication tells the extraordinary story of the health service. It gives a comprehensive overview of all the main landmarks, tracing achievements and breakthroughs in medicine, nursing, hospital development, and primary health care, in a way that combines both a clinical and a health management perspective.

ISBN 185717 148 9 1998 528pp £12.50

FORTHCOMING TITLES

SHAPING THE NEW NHS SERIES
Please note: titles and dates provisional at time of publication.

What is the Real Cost of More Patient Choice?
John Appleby, Anthony Harrison, Nancy Devlin

At first glance, more patient choice seems unequivocally 'a good thing'. But what trade-offs are really involved – and what price are we prepared to pay? How far can individual freedoms be extended while still retaining the essential objectives of the NHS? This paper lays out the questions the Government must answer if it wants to place patient choice at the heart of a taxpayer-funded health care system, including how extra costs will be met, whether patients are willing and able to exercise choice in their own best interests, and what kinds of limits to choice might be needed. It shows that, at the heart of the debate, we need to decide whether choice is a means to an end or an end in itself.

ISBN 185717 473 9 May 2003 52pp £6.50
Free download at www.kingsfundbookshop.org.uk

Is there a Role for an 'Arm's-length' NHS Agency?

Many people feel that politicians are still too involved in the day-to-day working of the NHS. This paper launches an important debate about whether the health service should continue to be directly managed by the Department of Health, and asks whether an 'arm's length' body with a semi-independent status similar to the BBC might be able to create more space for public, patients and professionals to improve health care.

ISBN 185717 474 7 2003 £6.50
Free download at www.kingsfundbookshop.org.uk

What Future for Medical Professionalism?

Recent debates such as the proposed changes to GPs' and consultants' contracts have raised important questions about the rights and obligations of doctors. Are we witnessing a sea change in the old professional values on which the NHS was built, and will medical staff of the future work to a very different 'psychological contract'? This paper opens up the debate, and argues that greater clarity about the role of professionals will be crucial to a constructive discussion about the direction of health care reform and improving the patient experience.

ISBN 185717 475 5 Autumn 2003 £6.50
Free download at www.kingsfundbookshop.org.uk

How Will Growing Pressures on Chronic Care be Managed?

How will the future NHS provide an effective response to growing demands for chronic care? Sharper market incentives – such as allowing funding to follow the patient's choice of provider, and encouraging more competition among providers, including those from the private sector – are being introduced. But these kinds of incentive seem more suitable for patients who are willing and able to travel to alternative providers for elective care, rather than patients who are old, frail and have complex chronic conditions. In the USA, managed care organisations offer excellent care for patients with chronic diseases in a competitive market. This paper asks what lessons the NHS can learn from their experience.

ISBN 185717 476 3 2003